2ND & 3RD D

FOOTBALL GROUNDS

BEFORE AND AFTER TAYLOR

Photography
by
Kevin Norminton & Chris Ambler

CONTENTS

FOREWORD

In 1990 we published a book entitled 'Full Colour Views of Football League Grounds' which was the first-ever book featuring full-colour ground photographs of all 92 Football League Grounds (photographs by Chris Ambler).

Since then the F.A. Carling Premiership has come into existence changing the face of English football dramatically. In addition, Lord Justice Taylor's Report on Football Ground Safety has highlighted the potential dangers of non-seated grounds and it is now a legal requirement for Premiership and 1st Division Football Grounds to be all-seaters.

During the Summer of 1995 and early in 1996, Mr. Kevin Norminton undertook the mammoth task of photographing the 48 grounds of the 2nd and 3rd Division clubs and the 44 grounds of the Premiership and 1st Division Clubs.

Readers will realise that three of the clubs which were in the League in 1990 are no longer around; Aldershot FC and Maidstone United FC having folded and Halifax Town FC having been relegated. In addition, their places have been taken by Colchester United FC (who had dropped to the Conference in 1990), together with Barnet FC and Wycombe Wanderers FC who were promoted as Conference Champions. For completeness, we have included all six of these clubs to show a complete 'now and then' picture of the grounds.

A few clubs, of course, have (through lack of resources) made little or no changes to their grounds but, on the whole, we feel that the changes which have been made reflect very creditably upon the smaller clubs of the Football League.

Copies of 'Premiership and 1st Division Football Grounds Before and After Taylor' are still available priced £9.99 per copy (post free if ordered from our address on page 100).

A further book covering the Scottish Grounds is being collated at the time of publication.

John Robinson
EDITOR

BLACKPOOL FC

Bloomfield Road - before the Taylor Report

BLACKPOOL FC

Bloomfield Road - after the Taylor Report

AFC BOURNEMOUTH
Dean Court - before the Taylor Report

AFC BOURNEMOUTH

Dean Court - after the Taylor Report

BRADFORD CITY FC

Valley Parade - before the Taylor Report

BRADFORD CITY FC

Valley Parade - after the Taylor Report

BRENTFORD FC

Griffin Park - before the Taylor Report

BRENTFORD FC

Griffin Park - after the Taylor Report

BRIGHTON & HOVE ALBION FC

Goldstone Ground - before the Taylor Report

BRIGHTON & HOVE ALBION FC

Goldstone Ground - after the Taylor Report

BRISTOL CITY FC

Ashton Gate - before the Taylor Report

BRISTOL CITY FC

Ashton Gate - after the Taylor Report

BRISTOL ROVERS FC

Twerton Park, Bath - before the Taylor Report

BRISTOL ROVERS FC

Twerton Park, Bath - after the Taylor Report

BURNLEY FC

Turf Moor - before the Taylor Report

BURNLEY FC

Turf Moor - after the Taylor Report

BURY FC
Gigg Lane - before the Taylor Report

BURY FC

Gigg Lane - after the Taylor Report

CAMBRIDGE UNITED FC

Abbey Stadium - before the Taylor Report

CAMBRIDGE UNITED FC

Abbey Stadium - after the Taylor Report

CARDIFF CITY FC

Ninian Park - before the Taylor Report

CARDIFF CITY FC

Ninian Park - after the Taylor Report

CARLISLE UNITED FC

Brunton Park - before the Taylor Report

CARLISLE UNITED FC
Brunton Park - after the Taylor Report

CHESTER CITY FC

Moss Rose Ground, Macclesfield - before the Taylor Report

CHESTER CITY FC

The Deva Stadium - after the Taylor Report (New Stadium)

CHESTERFIELD FC

Recreation Ground, Saltergate - before the Taylor Report

CHESTERFIELD FC

Recreation Ground, Saltergate - after the Taylor Report

CREWE ALEXANDRA FC

Gresty Road Ground - before the Taylor Report

CREWE ALEXANDRA FC

Gresty Road Ground - after the Taylor Report

DARLINGTON FC

Feethams Ground - before the Taylor Report

DARLINGTON FC

Feethams Ground - after the Taylor Report

DONCASTER ROVERS FC

Belle Vue - before the Taylor Report

DONCASTER ROVERS FC

Belle Vue - after the Taylor Report

EXETER CITY FC

St. James Park - before the Taylor Report

EXETER CITY FC

St. James Park - after the Taylor Report

FULHAM FC

Craven Cottage - before the Taylor Report

FULHAM FC

Craven Cottage - after the Taylor Report

GILLINGHAM FC

Priestfield Stadium - before the Taylor Report

GILLINGHAM FC

Priestfield Stadium - after the Taylor Report

HARTLEPOOL UNITED FC
Victoria Ground - before the Taylor Report

HARTLEPOOL UNITED FC

Victoria Ground - after the Taylor Report

HEREFORD UNITED FC

Edgar Street - before the Taylor Report

HEREFORD UNITED FC

Edgar Street - after the Taylor Report

HULL CITY FC

Boothferry Park - before the Taylor Report

HULL CITY FC

Boothferry Park - after the Taylor Report

LEYTON ORIENT FC

Leyton Stadium, Brisbane Road - before the Taylor Report

LEYTON ORIENT FC

Leyton Stadium, Brisbane Road - after the Taylor Report

LINCOLN CITY FC

Sincil Bank - before the Taylor Report

LINCOLN CITY FC

Sincil Bank - after the Taylor Report

MANSFIELD TOWN FC

Field Mill Ground, Quarry Lane - before the Taylor Report

MANSFIELD TOWN FC

Field Mill Ground, Quarry Lane - after the Taylor Report

NORTHAMPTON TOWN FC

County Ground - before the Taylor Report

NORTHAMPTON FC

Sixfields Stadium - after the Taylor Report (New Stadium)

NOTTS COUNTY FC

Meadow Lane - before the Taylor Report

NOTTS COUNTY FC

Meadow Lane - after the Taylor Report

OXFORD UNITED FC

Manor Ground - before the Taylor Report

OXFORD UNITED FC
Manor Ground - after the Taylor Report

PETERBOROUGH UNITED FC

London Road - before the Taylor Report

PETERBOROUGH UNITED FC

London Road - after the Taylor Report

PLYMOUTH ARGYLE FC

Home Park - before the Taylor Report

PLYMOUTH ARGYLE FC

Home Park - after the Taylor Report

PRESTON NORTH END FC

Deepdale - before the Taylor Report

PRESTON NORTH END FC

Deepdale - after the Taylor Report

ROCHDALE FC

Willbutts Lane, Spotland - before the Taylor Report

ROCHDALE FC

Willbutts Lane, Spotland - after the Taylor Report

ROTHERHAM UNITED FC

Millmoor Ground - before the Taylor Report

ROTHERHAM UNITED FC

Millmoor Ground - after the Taylor Report

SCARBOROUGH FC

McCain Stadium - before the Taylor Report

SCARBOROUGH FC

McCain Stadium - after the Taylor Report

SCUNTHORPE UNITED FC

Glanford Park - before the Taylor Report

SCUNTHORPE UNITED FC

Glanford Park - after the Taylor Report

SHREWSBURY TOWN FC

Gay Meadow - before the Taylor Report

SHREWSBURY TOWN FC

Gay Meadow - after the Taylor Report

STOCKPORT COUNTY FC

Edgeley Park - before the Taylor Report

STOCKPORT COUNTY FC

Edgeley Park - after the Taylor Report

SWANSEA CITY FC

Vetch Field - before the Taylor Report

SWANSEA CITY FC

Vetch Field - after the Taylor Report

SWINDON TOWN FC

County Ground - before the Taylor Report

SWINDON TOWN FC

County Ground - after the Taylor Report

TORQUAY UNITED FC

Plainmoor Ground - before the Taylor Report

TORQUAY UNITED FC

Plainmoor Ground - after the Taylor Report

WALSALL FC
Bescot Stadium - before the Taylor Report

WALSALL FC

Bescot Stadium - after the Taylor Report

WIGAN ATHLETIC FC

Springfield Park - before the Taylor Report

WIGAN ATHLETIC FC

Springfield Park - after the Taylor Report

WREXHAM FC

Racecourse Ground, Mold Road - before the Taylor Report

WREXHAM FC

Racecourse Ground, Mold Road - after the Taylor Report

YORK CITY FC

Bootham Crescent - before the Taylor Report

YORK CITY FC

Bootham Crescent - after the Taylor Report

ALDERSHOT FC

Recreation Ground - before the Taylor Report

HALIFAX TOWN FC

Shay Ground - before the Taylor Report

MAIDSTONE UNITED FC

Watling Street, Dartford - before the Taylor Report

BARNET FC
Underhill Stadium - after the Taylor Report

COLCHESTER UNITED FC

Layer Road Ground - before the Taylor Report

WYCOMBE WANDERERS FC

Adams Park - after the Taylor Report

ACKNOWLEDGEMENTS

We wish to thank all 48 Endsleigh Football League 2nd & 3rd Division clubs for their cooperation in the publication of this book.

In addition, we are indebted to Dixons Stores Group (Grimsby Branch) for providing film and processing for the 1995/96 photographs.

Finally our thanks go to Kevin Norminton and Chris Ambler for providing the photographs themselves.

British Library Cataloguing in Publication Data

A catalogue record for this book is available from the British Library

ISBN 0-947808-84-1

Copyright © 1996; SOCCER BOOK PUBLISHING LTD. (01472-696226)
72, St. Peters' Avenue, Cleethorpes, Sth. Humberside, DN35 8HU, England

Printed by The Polar Print Group, Leicester